PROSPERITY
BIBLE
BOOK OF MAGIC

UNLOCKING **ABUNDANCE** & **PROSPERITY**

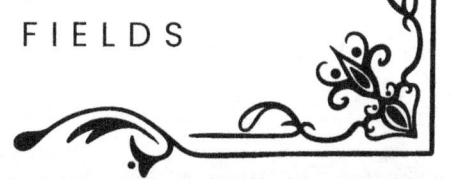

BY GEORGE W. FIELDS

All rights reserved. This book or any portion of it may not be reproduced or used in any manner whatsoever without express written permission of the publisher except for the use of brief quotations in a book review.

© 2024 George W. Fields. All rights reserved.

The Publisher has strived to be as accurate and complete as possible in the creation of this report, notwithstanding the fact that he does not warrant or represent at any time that the contents within are accurate due to the rapidly changing nature of the Internet.

The Publisher will not be responsible for any losses or damages of any kind incurred by the reader whether directly or indirectly arising from the use of the information found in this report.

This report is not intended for use as a source of legal, business, accounting, or financial advice. All readers are advised to seek the services of competent professionals in the legal, business, accounting, and finance fields.

No guarantees of income are made. The reader assumes responsibility for the use of the information contained herein. The author reserves the right to make changes without notice. The Publisher assumes no responsibility or liability whatsoever on behalf of the reader of this report.

TABLE OF CONTENTS

CHAPTER 1

The Boundless Potential of The Law of Attraction — 8

CHAPTER 2

Illuminating The Path: Setting Financial Goals — 13

CHAPTER 3

Unleashing The Power Within: Visualizing Financial Success — 17

CHAPTER 4

The Dance of Manifestation: Taking Bold Action — 21

TABLE OF CONTENTS

CHAPTER 5

transmuting Obstacles: Triumph Over Adversity

25

CHAPTER 6

Nurturing a Positive Mindset: Illuminating The Soul

29

CHAPTER 7

The Magic Unveiled: A Step-by-Step Guide to Attracting More Money

32

CHAPTER 8

The Art of Sigils: Amplifying the Law of Attraction

36

TABLE OF CONTENTS

CHAPTER 9 — 40

The Charms of Prosperous Herbs: Enchanted Herbs of Abundance

CHAPTER 10 — 45

The Universal Laws: The Enigmatic Tapestry of Universal Laws

CHAPTER 11 — 49

Mystical Crystals and the Dance of Wealth

CHAPTER 12 — 54

The Dance of Chi: Harnessing Feng Shui's Wealth

TABLE OF CONTENTS

CHAPTER 13

The Alkaline Path to Abundance: The Ascendancy of Alkaline Foods

59

CHAPTER 14

The Prosperous Path of Exercise: The Way of The Warrior

62

CHAPTER 15

The Tao of Abundance: Harnessing The Power of Taoism

65

CHAPTER 16

The Wisdom of Solomon and Thoth

69

TABLE OF CONTENTS

CHAPTER 17

Cosmic Blueprints: Unveiling The Secrets of Astrology, Numerology, and HD

73

CHAPTER 18

The Interplay of Spirituality, Religion, and Science

76

CHAPTER 19

The Final Curtain Falls

86

INTRODUCTION

Welcome to the enchanting realm where magic intertwines with boundless opportunities for prosperity and success. Within the sacred pages of this book lies a transformative journey as we delve into the mysteries of wealth and achievement, both within ourselves and the universe. As you open this mystical tome, a world of opulence unfolds before your eyes. The air is filled with the comforting aroma of freshly baked bread, and joyous laughter echoes through the surroundings. In this realm of sparkling grandeur, you are embraced by a community that embodies happiness, health, and affluence. This is the realm of the Opulence Law—a world where dreams materialize, and all things are possible through the power of ideas and aspirations. According to this law, every individual is entitled to prosperity and can manifest their deepest desires by harnessing the force of their thoughts and intentions.

To guide us on this journey into the realm of Opulence Law, we draw inspiration from timeless classics that have shaped the foundations of prosperity consciousness:

1. *"The Secret" by Rhonda Byrne* reveals the Law of Attraction, showing us how to harness the magnetic power of our thoughts and emotions. By cultivating a mindset of abundance and gratitude, we unlock the floodgates of prosperity, allowing our deepest desires to manifest effortlessly.
2. *"The Law of Attraction" by Esther and Jerry Hicks* expands our understanding of this universal law. Through the teachings of Abraham, we recognize that we are vibrational beings in a vibrational universe. By aligning our thoughts and emotions with abundance, we set forth a powerful intention that draws prosperity into our lives.
3. *"The Abundance Book" by John Randolph Price* offers profound guidance on transforming scarcity into opulence. Embracing the principles of Divine Abundance, we open ourselves to the limitless flow of prosperity and dissolve limiting beliefs that hinder our progress.
4. *"The Prosperous Universe" by Deepak Chopra* invites us on an inner journey beyond the confines of the material world. Through spiritual wisdom and practical tools, we discover the alchemical secrets that transform our consciousness into a vessel of abundance.
5. *"Think and Grow Rich" by Napoleon Hill*, a timeless classic, leads us through the corridors of success. By unearthing the principles of achievement, Hill imparts the secrets of the world's most successful individuals. Aligning our thoughts with

prosperity and fortifying our desires with unwavering determination, we unlock the vaults of abundance within us.

These sublime works will serve as our beacons, illuminating the path to prosperity and demonstrating that abundance is not a distant dream but a tangible reality within our grasp. The Prosperity Bible Book of Magic is a step-by-step manual that empowers us to incorporate the Law of Opulence into our daily lives. By harnessing the power of intention, we can align our thoughts and actions with abundance. By forging a positive and mindful relationship with money, we can use it to effect positive change. And by embracing a giving and receiving mindset with open hearts, we initiate an unending circle of prosperity.

We challenge the scarcity mindset that has confined us for too long, as we immerse ourselves in the entrancing knowledge found within these pages. We embrace the truth that we are co-creators of our prosperous reality and designers of our destinies. The magic within us ignites with newfound knowledge and power, illuminating the darkest corners of our lives with the flames of abundance.

If you find yourself facing financial challenges or feeling trapped by restrictive thoughts, fear not. I, too, was once in such a predicament, struggling with limited income and constant financial worries. However, as I delved into the Law of Opulence, I realized that my thoughts were the very barriers holding me back. By altering my mindset and behaviors, I gradually experienced an improvement in my financial situation, ultimately leading me to a life of abundance beyond my wildest dreams.

Now, I am living proof of the effectiveness of the Law of Opulence, and I want to extend an invitation to you. Join me on this journey to attract abundance into your life, as we use the Prosperity Bible Book of Magic as a powerful tool to unlock your full potential.

Within these pages, you will discover everything you need to know about the Law of Opulence and how it can manifest abundance in your life. You'll learn to identify and release limiting beliefs that hinder your progress. By cultivating an attitude of gratitude and abundance, you'll set forth precise intentions for your financial goals. And most importantly, you'll take inspired actions to propel yourself toward the prosperity you deserve.

Remember, you hold the power to design the life you desire, and the time to start is now. Let us create a world where all beings revel in happiness and abundance—a world where the symphony of magic and prosperity resonates with contentment and delight. Embrace the journey that awaits you on these pages, and let's embark together on a transformational path to luxury and riches.

The magic beckons and the time has come to answer the call.

Let's go!

FOREWORD

Dear Seekers of Abundance, Gather 'round and prepare to embark on an extraordinary journey that will reveal a treasure beyond measure. As your humble guide, I am honored to unveil the secrets that the universe has generously bestowed upon us. Within the enchanting realms of the Prosperity Bible Book of Magic, you will discover the boundless potential that resides within each soul. Financial triumph, a reality within your grasp, will unfold through the ethereal clasp of the law of attraction. Embrace patience, for true wealth is nurtured by the gentle grace of time. Let effort and dedication become your unwavering companions on this transformative voyage, shaping your destiny and illuminating the path you must tread.

I too have faced an immensely challenging financial circumstance in the past. Burdened with a $50,000 debt, no savings, and a failing car, I felt overwhelmed and despaired. However, fate brought me to the profound teachings of the law of attraction.

The law of attraction posits that whatever we focus our thoughts on, we attract more into our lives. With this newfound knowledge, I shifted my focus toward my financial goals. I visualized a life free of debt and filled with a comfortable savings account. I took proactive action by creating a budget and meticulously tracking my spending. Additionally, I sought out opportunities to increase my income.

Remarkably, within two years, I triumphantly paid off all my debt, acquired a new automobile, and built substantial savings. The profound impact of the law of attraction on my life left me astounded.

It is my firm belief that everyone can achieve financial prosperity. Within this book, I will share my journey to financial success, alongside the fundamental principles of the law of attraction that I utilized to transform my life.

I invite you to join me on this quest for financial achievement. Together, we have the power to accomplish anything we set our minds to.

Welcome to the Prosperity Bible Book of Magic!

Here, I implore you to put the law of attraction to the test. Begin by visualizing your financial objectives with unwavering clarity. Take the practical steps of creating a budget and diligently monitoring your expenses. Seek out innovative ways to increase your revenue. And most importantly, surround yourself with positive and supportive individuals who believe in your potential.

I believe in you wholeheartedly. I know that you can achieve financial success beyond your imagination.

Let us embark on this transformative journey together, hand in hand, as we unlock the magic of prosperity within ourselves.

With utmost sincerity and encouragement, let's do this!

CHAPTER ONE

The Boundless Potential of The Law Of Attraction

Prologue

In the vast expanse of the universe, where endless possibilities reside, a hidden force calls out to us, urging us to explore the depths of its power. Rhonda Byrne's "The Secret" reveals the promise of the law of attraction, illuminating the profound truth that like attracts like in the cosmic dance of existence. As we venture into this cosmic symphony, Napoleon Hill's "Think and Grow Rich" imparts timeless wisdom, emphasizing the significance of mindset and positive thinking in attracting wealth and achieving our goals.

The law of attraction assures us of this profound connection. According to this universal principle, opposites attract, which means that when we prioritize having joyful thoughts and feelings, we magnetize favorable circumstances into our lives.

On the contrary, focusing on negative thoughts and emotions draws more of the same into our reality.

The law of attraction is not a magical wand, guaranteeing instant success. Instead, it is a potent tool that, if used with dedication and effort, can assist us in reaching our objectives.

Introduction

The universe, a canvas of boundless wonders, resonates with the teachings of Esther Hicks and Jerry Hicks in "Ask and It Is Given: Learning to Manifest Your Desires." Their profound insights shed light on the law of attraction, guiding us to align our thoughts and emotions with our deepest desires. In Wayne W. Dyer's "The Power of Intention," we journey into the realm of intention and discover its pivotal role in shaping our reality. These profound works unravel the enigma of the law of attraction, inviting us to unlock its boundless potential.

The universe, dear friends, brims with infinite might, Whispers wise Napoleon Hill in celestial light. The law of attraction is not a mere magic fair, But a cosmic principle, in existence we share. Thoughts and emotions, vibrations in the astral air, Summon corresponding experiences, beyond compare.

My Personal Experiences with the Law of Attraction

As I embarked on my writing journey, doubts clouded my path, until I encountered the transformative power of the law of attraction. Drawing inspiration from "The Secret," I shifted my focus to positive thoughts and feelings, envisioning myself as a successful author. Gratitude filled my heart for the opportunities to share my work, aligning my vibration with abundance. Through the lens of Esther Hicks and Jerry Hicks' teachings, I witnessed the manifestation of my dreams. Positive feedback poured in, and the doors to publication swung open, validating the role of the law of attraction in my success.

How to Use the Law of Attraction Effectively

Guided by the principles laid out in "Think and Grow Rich," I learned to set clear goals and amplify their potency. With clarity, I painted vivid mental pictures of achieving my aspirations, as suggested in "The Power of Intention." Aligning my thoughts and emotions with my desires, I opened the gateway for the law of attraction to work its magic. As "Ask and It Is Given" taught, I stayed positive, swiftly dismissing negativity that threatened to derail my journey. Taking inspired action, no matter how small, I aligned my efforts with my goals. Patience became my ally, as I trusted in the timing of the universe, knowing that the law of attraction would yield its fruits in due course.

While the law of attraction remains an ever-unfolding mystery, scientific studies have begun to shed light on its potential.

Rhonda Byrne's "The Secret" echoes findings that positive thoughts about health can aid in recovery, substantiating the connection between mindset and well-being. Furthermore, the research highlighted in "Ask and It Is Given" unveils the efficacy of visualization techniques in bolstering success rates. Although scientific evidence is still limited, these studies hint at the existence of a real phenomenon behind the law of attraction.

Although the law of attraction is a straightforward idea, it can be challenging to comprehend. You can apply the law of attraction more effectively if you follow the recommendations below:

1. **Establish precise objectives**. Be clear and detailed about what you hope to accomplish. Instead of saying "I want to be successful," it is more beneficial to state "I am a published novelist who earns $100,000 per year."
2. **Visualize your goals**. Envision your achievements vividly, using all your senses. What does success sound like? What sensations do you experience? What thoughts run through your mind? Who are you with?
3. **Stay positive**. Focus on the positive aspects of your life and aspirations. Before letting go of negative thoughts, acknowledge them, and then shift your focus to positivity.

Conclusion

The law of attraction, as explored through the wisdom of "The Secret," "Think and Grow Rich," "Ask and It Is Given," and "The Power of Intention," stands as a potent tool for achieving our goals.

It is not a mere magic wand but a force that responds to our thoughts, emotions, and actions. By aligning our energy with our desires and working diligently towards them, we can tap into the boundless potential of the law of attraction. With unwavering belief and persistence, we hold the key to manifesting our dreams and shaping a life of abundance.

Additional Thoughts

As we continue on our path, Joe Vitale's "The Attractor Factor: 5 Simple Steps for Generating Money (or Anything Else) From the Inside Out" provides insightful advice on using the law of attraction to attract financial abundance. Along with the foundational literature mentioned earlier, these works weave a rich tapestry of information that enlightens us on how to fully comprehend and use the law of attraction.

Remember, the law of attraction can be applied to any goal, whether it be financial success or nurturing interpersonal relationships. However, it cannot replace diligent effort. To achieve your goals, you must continue to work hard.

The law of attraction is a potent tool for personal development. You have the power to harness its magic and create the life you desire.

CHAPTER TWO
Illuminating the Path: Setting Financial Goals

Introduction

In the vast expanse of the universe, lies the power to manifest our deepest desires. The principles of goal-setting, supported by timeless wisdom, illuminate the path to financial success. Drawing inspiration from influential books such as "New Directions in Goal-Setting Theory" by Edwin A. Locke and Gary P. Latham, "Mindset: The New Psychology of Success" by Carol S. Dweck, and "Emotional Intelligence: A Science-Based Approach" edited by Gerald Matthews, Moshe Zeidner, and Richard D. Roberts, and finding guidance from the achievements of the great Benjamin Franklin in his autobiography, we can align our intentions with the limitless potential of the universe.

Psychological research extensively supports the efficacy of goal-setting as a strategy for achieving success, as highlighted in

"New Directions in Goal-Setting Theory." Studies have shown that setting specific and challenging goals enhances performance and motivation, increasing the likelihood of achieving desired outcomes. These findings, along with the principles outlined by Locke and Latham, provide a solid scientific foundation for harnessing the power of goal-setting on our financial journey.

The Importance of Setting Financial Goals

Drawing upon the insights from Carol S. Dweck's "Mindset: The New Psychology of Success," we recognize the significance of setting financial goals in attracting abundance into our lives. Specific financial goals provide direction, focus, and motivation, aligning our thoughts and actions with our desired outcomes. By integrating Dweck's teachings on the power of a growth mindset, we embrace the belief that our financial circumstances are not fixed but can be improved through effort, learning, and perseverance.

Specific, Measurable, Achievable, Relevant, and Time-Bound Goals

When setting financial objectives, it is essential to ensure they are precise and well-defined. Avoid vague aspirations and concentrate on what you truly want with specificity. For instance, instead of expressing, "I want to be rich," be more specific about your desired net worth. Furthermore, make sure that your financial goals are measurable. This enables you to monitor your progress and assess your success as you move forward. Establish checkpoints or milestones to gauge your advancement toward your objectives.

It is equally crucial to set achievable goals. While it is important to dream big, setting unrealistic objectives can lead to disappointment and discouragement. Strike a balance between ambition and reality.

Moreover, your financial objectives should be aligned with your values, aspirations, and overall vision for your life. This ensures that your goals are relevant and meaningful to you.

Lastly, adopt a time-bound approach. Establish deadlines for achieving your financial goals, as Benjamin Franklin did in his autobiography. Having clear timelines creates a sense of urgency and accountability, propelling you toward your objectives.

The Importance of Having a Clear Vision

Drawing inspiration from the autobiography of Benjamin Franklin, we understand the significance of having a clear vision of our financial future. Franklin's meticulous planning and detailed envisioning of his goals served as a guiding light, fueling his motivation and focus. By incorporating visualization techniques, as discussed in "Emotional Intelligence," we vividly imagine our ideal financial reality, encompassing all aspects of lifestyle, possessions, and experiences. This clarity of vision strengthens our belief in its attainment and propels us forward on our financial journey.

How to Set Financial Goals

Integrating the wisdom from these influential books, we outline a step-by-step approach to setting financial goals. Drawing upon the insights from "New Directions in Goal-Setting Theory," we emphasize the importance of brainstorming a list of goals, prioritizing them based on feasibility and importance, and transforming them into specific and measurable statements. The teachings of Carol S. Dweck encourage us to maintain a growth mindset and stay positive as we set our financial goals. Displaying our goals in a visible place, as advocated in "Emotional Intelligence," reinforces our commitment and serves as a constant reminder of our aspirations. Regular review and adjustment, as outlined by the principles of goal-setting, ensure that our financial goals remain aligned with our evolving circumstances and aspirations.

1. **Brainstorm**: Start by brainstorming a list of your financial goals. Consider what you want to achieve financially and the lifestyle you desire.
2. **Prioritize**: Once you have a list of goals, prioritize them based on their importance and feasibility. Determine which goals you can realistically achieve soon.
3. **Specific and Measurable**: Transform your goals into specific and measurable statements. Define them in precise terms, quantifying the desired outcome.
4. **Write and Display**: Write down your financial goals and keep them in a visible place as a constant reminder. This practice reinforces your commitment and motivates consistent action.

5. **Review and Adjust**: Regularly review your goals and assess your progress. Adjust them as necessary to align with changing circumstances or newfound clarity.

Conclusion

By following these steps and adhering to the principles of effective goal-setting, you can set yourself up for success on your financial journey. The wisdom and achievements of figures like Benjamin Franklin make him an excellent historical figure to compare this chapter to in terms of success, emphasizing the significance of goal-setting strategies and personal growth on the path to financial abundance.

CHAPTER THREE
Unleashing the Power Within: Visualizing Financial Success

Introduction

Step into the realm of visualization, a mystical practice that bridges the gap between dreams and tangible manifestations. Within this ethereal realm, we can bring our desired outcomes to life through vivid mental landscapes. Engage all your senses in this enchanting dance of creation, where opulence becomes visible, prosperity echoes in your ears, and the vibrant energy of success is within your grasp. Draw inspiration from the wisdom and practices of figures who harnessed the power of visualization, such as the legendary basketball player Michael Jordan.

The power of visualization has been extensively studied in sports psychology, demonstrating significant benefits for performance enhancement. Jon Paul Crimi's book, "The Power of Visualization: Meditation Secrets That Matter the Most," explores the transformative power of visualization and provides practical techniques to harness its potential in various aspects of life, including finances. It delves into the scientific evidence supporting visualization as a tool for achieving success.

In this chapter, we delve into the transformative power of visualization in manifesting financial success. We explore how creating detailed mental images of achieving financial goals, incorporating all the senses, can make the visualizations vivid and impactful. We also suggest the use of affirmations and vision boards to further support the visualization process.

The Importance of Visualization for Financial Success

Visualization is a potent tool that can help you attract more abundance into your life. Drawing from the insights of Shakti Gawain's book, "Creative Visualization: Use the Power of Your Imagination to Create What You Want in Your Life," we delve into the practice of creative visualization and its role in manifesting desires. It emphasizes the importance of creating detailed mental images of achieving financial goals and incorporating all the senses to make the visualizations vivid and impactful.

Techniques for Effective Visualization

To effectively utilize visualization for financial abundance, follow the insights from Jim Afremow's book, "The Champion's Mind: How Great Athletes Think, Train, and Thrive." While primarily focused on athletes, this book highlights the importance of visualization and mental rehearsal in achieving peak performance. Apply these principles to your financial success journey.

1. **Be Specific**: Clearly define your financial goals and the lifestyle you desire. Visualize yourself achieving these goals with precise detail.
2. **Engage All Your Senses**: Incorporate all your senses into your visualizations. See, hear, touch, smell, and feel the emotions associated with achieving your financial objectives.
3. **Make It Feel Real**: Make your visualizations feel as real as possible. Draw inspiration from Michael Jordan's practice of vividly imagining success before stepping onto the court.
4. **Practice Regularly**: Visualization is a catalyst, not a standalone solution. Practice regularly and consistently, combining visualization with real-world efforts towards your financial goals.

Example of a Visualization Exercise:

1. **Find a Quiet Space**: Locate a peaceful area where you won't be disturbed.
2. **Deep Breathing**: Breathe deeply for a few breaths to calm your body and mind.
3. **Close Your Eyes**: Shut your eyes and mentally see yourself accomplishing your financial objectives. Watch as the life you want unfolds in front of you.
4. **Engage Your Senses**: Embrace the experience with all your senses engaged. Listen to the sounds, experience the sensations, and feel the emotions of success.

5. **Gradual Return**: Open your eyes gradually and give yourself some time to center yourself in the present.

Additional Tips

1. **Use Affirmations**: Instill empowering thoughts in your subconscious mind regarding money and financial success. Repetition of positive affirmations will help reinforce these beliefs.
2. **Create a Vision Board**: Craft a vision board with pictures, words, and phrases that symbolize your financial objectives. Place it somewhere you'll see it frequently to maintain focus and motivation.
3. **Take Action**: Remember that visualization is a catalyst, not a standalone remedy. Combine your visualizations with real-world action toward your financial goals.

Conclusion

By drawing insights from these books and integrating their teachings into your practice, you can unlock the transformative power of visualization and propel yourself toward greater financial abundance. Embrace the realm of visualization, harness your imagination, and immerse yourself in the sensory experience of achieving your financial goals. With dedication, consistency, and a vivid vision of success, you can manifest the financial abundance you desire.

CHAPTER FOUR

The Dance of Manifestation: Taking Bold Action

Introduction

To engage in a harmonious dance with the universe, one must move with purpose and grace, embracing the power of bold action. It is through taking decisive steps aligned with your financial goals that you invite prosperity into your life. Consistency becomes the currency of success, radiating its brilliance as you persevere on your journey. In moments of uncertainty, summon your true courage, for it is through boldness that you unleash your innate power and virtue. Just as historical figures like Thomas Edison and J.K. Rowling harnessed the power of action to achieve their dreams. We, too, can draw inspiration from their achievements and the wisdom shared in books that explore the transformative power of taking bold action.

The Importance of Taking Action

Angela Duckworth examines the critical importance of consistent effort and action in accomplishing long-term goals in her book "Grit: The Power of Passion and Perseverance." She emphasizes the significance of having a growth mindset, resilience, and the will to succeed in the face of challenges. Making progress and developing the character and mindset required for financial abundance go hand in hand when taking action.

Darren Hardy, in "The Compound Effect," emphasizes the power of consistent action, no matter how small, in creating significant results over time. By taking consistent steps toward our financial goals, we create a positive compounding effect that propels us forward. It is through daily actions, however small, that we build momentum and make progress toward our desired outcomes.

How to Take Action

James Clear's book "Atomic Habits" offers practical strategies for taking action and creating positive habits. Clear emphasizes the power of small, consistent actions and how they can compound over time to create remarkable outcomes. By focusing on small changes and incremental progress, we can make the process of taking action more manageable and sustainable. "The Slight Edge" by Jeff Olson reinforces the importance of consistent daily actions and their ability to lead to remarkable results over time. Olson emphasizes that success is not achieved overnight but through consistent, positive actions that accumulate and create a positive ripple effect in our lives.

Taking inspiration from Brian Tracy's "Eat That Frog!", we recognize the significance of tackling the most challenging tasks first. By taking bold action and addressing the most critical actions head-on, we build momentum, overcome procrastination, and create a sense of accomplishment that fuels further progress.

"The 12 Week Year" by Brian P. Moran and Michael Lennington introduces the concept of setting shorter, focused goals within a 12-week timeframe. By breaking down our financial goals into manageable chunks and committing to consistent action within a defined timeframe, we create a sense of urgency and accountability that propels us forward.

Additional Tips

In "The Happiness Advantage," Shawn Achor emphasizes the importance of celebrating small victories along the way. By acknowledging and appreciating our progress, we boost our motivation, positivity, and overall happiness, creating a virtuous cycle that fuels further action. "The Go-Giver" by Bob Burg and John David Mann highlights the power of giving and building relationships in achieving success. By taking bold action in helping and providing value to others, we create a network of support and opportunities that can contribute to our financial growth.

Conclusion

Taking action is essential for attracting more abundance into your life. The wisdom found in "Grit," "The Compound Effect," "Atomic Habits," "The Slight Edge," "Eat That Frog!," "The 12 Week Year," and "The Happiness Advantage" recognizes the transformative power of consistent, bold action on the path to financial success. By embracing the lessons from these books and embodying the perseverance and determination of historical figures like Thomas Edison and J.K. Rowling, we can unlock our innate potential and manifest our financial dreams. Remember, the law of attraction is a powerful tool, but it is through taking action that we turn our dreams into tangible realities.

CHAPTER FIVE

Transmuting Obstacles: Triumph Over Adversity

Introduction

Obstacles, like fleeting shadows on life's grand stage, may momentarily obscure our path. Yet, they are merely illusions, waiting to be conquered and engaged. Dear reader, fortify yourself with resilience as your armor and shield. Craft a strategic plan, and watch as your foes yield. Triumph over adversity with an undeterred spirit, rising above challenges like a resurgent phoenix. Just as historical figures like Nelson Mandela demonstrated remarkable resilience in the face of adversity, his triumphs inspire us to overcome obstacles on our journey to financial success.

Resilience and its Importance in the Journey to Financial Success

Resilience is a powerful psychological trait that enables individuals to bounce back from adversity and continue striving toward their goals. Numerous studies highlight the importance of resilience in achieving success and maintaining well-being in the face of challenges. Nelson Mandela's life serves as a poignant example of resilience in the pursuit of justice and transformation, reminding us that setbacks are not roadblocks but stepping stones toward growth.

Specific Examples of Obstacles

1. **Financial setbacks**: This could include losing a job, experiencing a medical emergency, or having to pay for unexpected expenses. Financial setbacks can be emotionally and mentally challenging, but with resilience, you can navigate these difficult times and find ways to rebuild and recover.
2. **Personal challenges**: This could include dealing with a mental or physical illness, caring for a family member, or experiencing a divorce or other major life changes. Personal challenges can disrupt your financial stability and create added stress, but resilience allows you to adapt and find new ways to manage your finances and maintain focus on your goals.
3. **External challenges**: This could include discrimination, prejudice, or other forms of social injustice. External challenges can hinder financial progress and create additional barriers, but resilience empowers you to advocate for change, seek support, and persevere in the face of adversity.

How to Deal with Setbacks

1. **Acknowledge your emotions**: After a setback, allow yourself to feel the emotions that arise. It's essential to process and acknowledge your feelings, giving yourself the space to grieve or reflect on what happened.
2. **Reframe setbacks as learning opportunities**: Every setback is a chance for learning and growth. Reflect on what went wrong and identify lessons that can be applied to future endeavors.
3. **Stay focused on the future**: While setbacks may be discouraging, avoid dwelling on the past. Focus on the opportunities and possibilities that lie ahead, and channel your energy into moving forward.
4. **Seek support**: Reach out to friends, family, or a professional support network to share your challenges and seek guidance. Having a supportive community can make a significant difference in navigating difficult times.
5. **Take small steps**: Break down your financial goals into manageable steps. Taking small actions consistently can build momentum and lead to significant progress over time.

Conclusion

Although the journey to financial success may present challenges, it is essential to embrace resilience and tenacity as guiding principles. Just as historical figures like Nelson Mandela faced seemingly insurmountable obstacles with unwavering determination, we too can harness our resilience to overcome adversity and continue on the path to financial abundance.

Remember, setbacks are part of the journey, but they do not define our destiny. Stay focused, stay resilient, and let the triumph over adversity be a testament to the strength of your spirit and the fulfillment of your financial dreams.

CHAPTER SIX
Nurturing a Positive Mindset: Illuminating the Soul

Introduction

Within thy being, a reservoir of radiant light, Nurture thy soul, with positivity ever so bright. Believe, dear reader, in thy ability profound, To manifest abundance, with every thought and sound. Gratitude, the elixir, shall attract miracles untold, Surround thyself with kindred spirits, and behold! Just as historical figures like Mahatma Gandhi embraced a positive mindset amidst adversity, their unwavering belief serves as a guiding light in nurturing our positive mindset on the path to financial success.

The Power of a Positive Mindset

A positive mindset is instrumental in attracting positive experiences and financial abundance into your life. By cultivating a positive outlook, you open the doors to new possibilities and opportunities.

Just as historical figures like Mahatma Gandhi demonstrated unwavering belief in themselves and their cause, embrace self-confidence and let it shine in all facets of your life.

Concentrate on the good: In challenging times, it is easy to focus on the negatives, but deliberately focus on the good things in your life. Draw inspiration from the tenacity and optimism of historical individuals like Mahatma Gandhi, who found strength in the face of adversity.

Embrace thankfulness: Develop your gratitude as a potent weapon for maintaining a happy outlook. When you express thanks for the blessings and opportunities in your life, you attract more goodness and abundance.

Harnessing the Power of Positive Affirmations

Practice positive affirmations by repeating empowering statements that align with your goals. These affirmations program your subconscious mind with positive thoughts and reinforce your belief in achieving financial abundance. For example, you might say to yourself, "I am a magnet for financial abundance. I attract money easily and effortlessly." Books like "You Can Heal Your Life" by Louise Hay delve into the power of affirmations for personal growth and transformation.

Visualizing Success

Engage in visualization exercises where you vividly imagine

yourself achieving your financial goals. As you visualize, see, hear, feel, and taste your success as if it were happening right now. This will help you to program your subconscious mind with the belief that success is already yours. "Creative Visualization" by Shakti Gawain offers techniques and practices for harnessing the power of visualization.

Taking Inspired Action

Action is a catalyst for maintaining a positive mindset. When you take purposeful steps towards your goals, you reinforce your capabilities, boost confidence, and keep your mindset positive. So don't just sit around and wait for things to happen. Take action today! "The 5 Second Rule" by Mel Robbins explores a simple yet powerful technique to overcome hesitation and take decisive action.

Conclusion

Nurturing a positive mindset is a continual dedication and a lifelong journey. Yet, if you choose to view things positively, you can prosper in life and accomplish your financial goals. Incorporate the advice in this chapter into your everyday routine and embrace a positive outlook. Believe in your abilities, adopt a positive mindset, and follow your motivation. Anything is possible with a positive outlook!

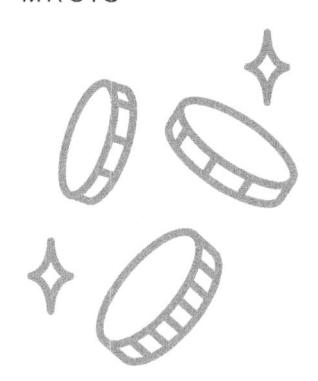

CHAPTER SEVEN

The Magic Unveiled: A Step-by-Step Guide to Attracting More Money

Introduction

Within the depths of your soul lies a hidden magic, waiting to be unveiled. This chapter provides a step-by-step guide to unlocking the secrets of attracting untold riches. Drawing wisdom from renowned books on personal development and financial success, such as The Secret by Rhonda Byrne, The Millionaire Mind by Thomas J. Stanley and William D. Danko. The Automatic Millionaire by David Bach, and The Richest Man in Babylon by George S. Clason. We embark on a journey of transformation. Together, we will explore essential concepts and practices that pave the way to financial abundance.

Step-by-Step Guide to Attracting More Money

1. Creating Definable Financial Objectives

Setting definite and defined financial goals is the first step in attracting more money.

What do you hope to accomplish financially? Do you intend to put money aside for a down payment on a home? Repay debt? Invest money for the future? You can begin creating a strategy to reach your objectives after you are clear on what you want.

Here are some pointers for establishing precise and detailed financial goals:
- Specify your objectives: Say "I want to save $10,000 in the following year" rather than "I want to save more money."
- Set quantifiable objectives: How will you know when your goal has been met? You may monitor your success, for instance, by setting monthly savings goals.

2. Embracing the Law of Attraction and Positive Thinking

The law of attraction asserts that like attracts like. By maintaining a positive mindset and focusing on your financial goals with unwavering belief, you can attract more money into your life. Surround yourself with positivity, express gratitude for the blessings in your life, and use affirmations to reinforce your belief in financial abundance.

3. Utilizing Visualization Techniques

Engage in visualization exercises regularly, vividly imagining yourself achieving your financial goals. See, hear, and feel your success as if it were happening in the present moment. This powerful practice helps program your subconscious mind with the belief that your goals are within reach.

4. Taking Inspired Action

Boldly take action toward your financial objectives, even if they seem daunting. Break down your goals into manageable steps and consistently work towards them. The combination of visualization and action is a potent force in attracting financial abundance.

5. Overcoming Obstacles

Triumph over adversity with resilience and a positive mindset. Challenges may arise on your journey to financial success, but view them as opportunities for growth and learning. Draw inspiration from historical figures and books that exemplify perseverance in the face of obstacles.

Conclusion

The secrets to attracting more money and achieving financial abundance lie within you. By following the step-by-step guide in this chapter, you can unlock the magic within and manifest your financial dreams. Embrace the law of attraction, set clear and defined financial goals, visualize your success, and take inspired action. Remember that challenges may arise, but with a positive mindset and unwavering determination, you can overcome them and pave the way to financial prosperity. Trust in the power of your thoughts, actions, and the universe, and you shall experience the enchanting dance of manifestation in your financial journey.

CHAPTER EIGHT
The Art of Sigils: Amplifying the Law of Attraction

Introduction

Sigils shall cast their spell, a fusion of divine, ancient wisdom, and modern tale to tell. Sacred symbols, encapsulating desires so true, amplify the law of attraction, as skies turn azure blue. With every stroke, intention imbued, we sing, beckoning wealth and abundance, with each sigil's wing.

As we delve into the art of sigils and their connection to the law of attraction. Let us draw inspiration from the historical figure of Helena Blavatsky, known for her deep understanding of esoteric wisdom and her ability to manifest her desires through spiritual practices.

While sigils may not have been studied scientifically, their use aligns with the principles of focused intention and symbolic representation of desires. In this chapter, we explore the art of sigils, discussing what they are, how they work, and how they can be utilized to attract more money into your life.

Understanding Sigils

Sigils are symbolic representations of desired outcomes, whether in the form of a drawing, word, or number. Helena Blavatsky utilized various symbols and sigils in her spiritual practices to manifest her desires and connect with higher realms of consciousness, as explored in "The Book of Sigil Magic" by Franz Bardon.

The Power of Sigils

Sigils operate through the law of attraction. By creating a sigil, you concentrate your intention and signal the universe about your desired outcome. This alignment with the universal energy allows the manifestation of your intentions, as explained in "Sigils: How to Create Your Own Magickal Tools" by Adam Blackthorne.

Creating a Sigil

While there are various approaches to creating sigils, the fundamental steps involve defining your desired outcome and brainstorming symbols or images that represent your desire. You can then combine them into a single sigil, as detailed in "The Complete Book of Magic and Witchcraft" by Raymond Buckland.

Charging and Releasing the Sigil

To enhance the power of your sigil, charge it with your intention through meditation, visualization, or mantra recitation. Helena Blavatsky's practices, as described in "The Secret Language of Symbols" by Jayne Gackenbach, involved spending dedicated time focusing on her sigils, channeling her energy and intention into them. Once charged, release the sigil into the universe, following the guidance provided in "Advanced Sigil Magic" by Gordon White.

Using Sigils for Financial Attraction

Sigils can be effectively used to attract money and financial abundance. It is crucial to be specific about your desired financial outcome, avoid symbols of lack or limitation, and infuse the sigil with your intention before releasing it into the universe. Explore the techniques and insights presented in the referenced books to optimize your practice.

Conclusion

Sigils offer a powerful means of manifesting desires, including financial abundance. Inspired by the practices of Helena Blavatsky and drawing wisdom from the references mentioned above, we have explored the art of sigils and their connection to the law of attraction. Remember that while sigil magic can enhance your financial situation, it is important to complement it with action and effort. By integrating the power of sigils with dedicated action, you can attract more money into your life and manifest your financial aspirations.

CHAPTER NINE

The Charms of Prosperous Herbs: Enchanted Herbs of Abundance

Introduction

Discover the mystical realm where prosperity and botanical enchantment intertwine. In this chapter, we delve into the secrets of ageless and pure herbs, unveiling their power to beckon riches and transcend time. These sacred herbs, steeped in ancient wisdom, hold the key to unlocking untold abundance. Embark on this enchanting journey, for within the ethereal embrace of these magical herbs lies the potential to transform your financial destiny. Drawing inspiration from the following references:

While scientific evidence supporting the specific effects of magic herbs on wealth attraction may be limited, studies suggest that certain herbs can have a positive impact on mental and emotional well-being, as explored in Scott Cunningham's "Cunningham's Encyclopedia of Magical Herbs."

How to Use Magic Herbs to Attract Money

1. **Carry a sacred herb as an amulet of attraction**: This is a traditional way to use herbs for financial success, as described in "Cunningham's Encyclopedia of Magical Herbs" by Scott Cunningham. Some popular herbs for attracting money include basil, cloves, ginger, lavender, marjoram, rosemary, cinnamon, and many more.

2. **Cultivate and nurture magical herbs in your garden**: This is a great way to surround yourself with the energy of prosperity. When you plant and care for these herbs, you are also planting the seeds of financial abundance in your life. Refer to "Cunningham's Encyclopedia of Magical Herbs" by Scott Cunningham for guidance on cultivating specific herbs.

3. **Prepare herb-infused teas and consume them before significant financial events**: This is a great way to align your energies with the desired outcome. For example, if you are going to a job interview, you could drink tea made with basil and rosemary to help you project confidence and competence, as suggested in "Cunningham's Encyclopedia of Magical Herbs" by Scott Cunningham.

4. **Ignite herb-infused incense**: This is a great way to create an aura of positivity and prosperity in your home or workspace. When you burn incense, the fragrant smoke carries the energy of the herbs into the air, creating a sacred space where financial abundance can flourish. Explore the recommendations in "Cunningham's Encyclopedia of Magical Herbs" by Scott Cunningham for suitable

herb combinations.

5. **Adorn your living and professional spaces with herb powders**: This is a subtle but effective way to attract money into your life. When you sprinkle herb powders around your home or office, you are sending a message to the universe that you are open to receiving financial abundance. Refer to "Cunningham's Encyclopedia of Magical Herbs" by Scott Cunningham for information on creating and using herb powders.

Herbs that Bring Wealth

- **Poppy Seeds**: Often associated with prosperity and believed by many to bring good luck, as mentioned in "Cunningham's Encyclopedia of Magical Herbs" by Scott Cunningham.

- **Lemongrass**: Known for its calming properties, it is believed by some to attract prosperity and has potential benefits for physical well-being, as highlighted in "Cunningham's Encyclopedia of Magical Herbs" by Scott Cunningham.

- **Cinnamon**: Revered for its aromatic allure and culinary uses, it is said to attract success, prosperity, and love, as well as promote healing and purification, as explored in "Cunningham's Encyclopedia of Magical Herbs" by Scott Cunningham.

- **Irish Moss**: Apart from its potential immune-boosting properties, some people believe that Irish moss can attract money and good fortune, as mentioned in "Cunningham's Encyclopedia of Magical Herbs" by Scott Cunningham.

- **Chamomile**: Known for its soothing effects, spraying the soil around the house with chamomile tea is said to open the door to prosperity and abundance, as noted in "Cunningham's Encyclopedia of Magical Herbs" by Scott Cunningham.

- **Cloves**: These aromatic flower buds are believed to possess aphrodisiac properties and are also associated with luck, love, and protection, as highlighted in "Cunningham's Encyclopedia of Magical Herbs" by Scott Cunningham.

Conclusion

The charms of prosperous herbs offer a potent and captivating means of enhancing your financial journey. We have explored the art of using magic herbs to attract wealth and prosperity, drawing wisdom from "Cunningham's Encyclopedia of Magical Herbs" by Scott Cunningham. Remember, magic herbs serve as catalysts, creating an atmosphere that harmonizes with the forces of prosperity. By integrating the power of the law of attraction, visualization, and the charms of these enchanted herbs, you can pave the way for a symphony of possibilities, illuminating the path toward the life you have always dreamed of.

Additional Tips

1. Choose herbs that resonate with your personal goals and intentions, referencing "Cunningham's Encyclopedia of Magical Herbs" by Scott Cunningham for guidance.
2. Use herbs in a way that feels authentic and meaningful to you, exploring various techniques described in the referenced book.
3. Be consistent with your use of herbs and visualization techniques, dedicating time and intention to your practice.
4. Trust the process and let go of any attachment to the outcome, allowing the universe to work its magic in its timing and manner.

CHAPTER TEN

The Universal Laws: The Enigmatic Tapestry of Universal Laws

Introduction

In the realm of the cosmic symphony, where secrets and wonders intertwine, lies the enigmatic tapestry of universal laws, divine. As Aristotle sought truth in metaphysics profoundly, these laws reveal the wisdom of the cosmos, where treasures abound. The Law of Vibration, harmonizing our souls' vibration with joy, and The Law of Correspondence, reflect the abundance in the world we deploy. With the Law of Cause and Effect, conscious actions we take, create ripples of prosperity, in every step we make. And the Law of Abundance, celebrating the universe's endless wealth, inviting opulence into our lives, and embracing infinite blessings with stealth. With clear intentions, aligned actions, and faith's unwavering might, we embrace the universal laws, weaving a tapestry of financial delight. Patience and persistence, gratitude and giving we hold dear, expanding knowledge, celebrating progress, banishing doubt and fear. Together, we dance in harmony, co-creating a life of prosperous glee, embracing the universal laws, and unlocking wealth's symphony.

Comparing the Universal Laws to the Philosophical Teachings of Aristotle

Aristotle was a renowned philosopher known for his investigation of metaphysics and natural philosophy. The universal laws, with their profound insights into the operation of the world, find resonance with his philosophical teachings. The universal rules give us a window into the rich tapestry that regulates our life, just as Aristotle attempted to comprehend the fundamental principles underpinning the cosmos.

- **The Law of Vibration**: This mystical law aligns with Aristotle's exploration of the vibrational nature of reality. As Aristotle contemplated the harmonious interplay of vibrations in the cosmos, the Law of Vibration reminds us to attune ourselves to high vibrations of positivity, gratitude, and joy. By harmonizing our vibration with the abundant flow of the universe, we open ourselves to untold riches. Drawing inspiration from "The Law of Vibration" by Tony Plummer.

- **The Law of Correspondence**: Aristotle's belief in the interconnectedness of all things finds resonance with the Law of Correspondence. Just as Aristotle saw the reflection of truth in the natural world, this law reminds us that our inner alignment with abundance is mirrored in our external reality.

By cultivating inner harmony and aligning our thoughts and emotions with prosperity, we witness its reflection in the world around us. Referencing "The Kybalion: A Study of The Hermetic Philosophy of Ancient Egypt and Greece" by Three Initiates.

- **The Law of Cause and Effect**: Aristotle's understanding of causality and the principle of action and reaction aligns with the Law of Cause and Effect. This law reminds us that our actions carry consequences, and by choosing actions aligned with wealth and abundance, we create a ripple effect that brings forth abundant fruits. Through conscious and purposeful actions, we pave the way for financial success. Drawing insights from "The Science of Getting Rich" by Wallace D. Wattles.

- **The Law of Abundance**: Aristotle's belief in the inherent abundance of the universe resonates with the Law of Abundance. Just as Aristotle celebrated the vastness and richness of the cosmos, this law invites us to open our hearts to the boundless flow of abundance. By embracing the limitless nature of the universe, we align ourselves with its infinite blessings and allow opulence to grace our lives. Referencing "The Law of Attraction: The Basics of the Teachings of Abraham" by Esther Hicks and Jerry Hicks.

Conclusion

The universal laws, akin to Shakespearean sonnets lighting the way to wisdom, hold profound insights into the nature of the cosmos and our place within it. As we immerse ourselves in their teaching and surrender to their divine dance, financial abundance adorns our life's play. Just as Aristotle sought to understand the fundamental principles of existence, we too can embrace these universal laws, integrating their wisdom into our lives. By nurturing unwavering faith, applying their teachings, and allowing the symphony of prosperity to echo through every aspect of our lives, we weave a grand tapestry adorned with the splendors of abundance.

CHAPTER ELEVEN

Mystical Crystals and the Dance of Wealth

Introduction

In the realm of time, crystals shimmer with untold secrets, captivating seekers of wealth. Like ancient gemstones revered for their mystical qualities, crystals hold the power to manifest financial abundance. While scientific evidence continues to unfold, studies suggest that crystals can promote relaxation, enhance focus, and reduce stress. Moldavite awakens intuition and attracts success, Citrine beckons prosperity, Pyrite unveils hidden fortunes, Green Aventurine manifests dreams, Clear Quartz amplifies intentions, and Amethyst guards wealth. By carrying crystals, placing them strategically, meditating with them, and cleansing and programming their energy, we can align ourselves with the energetic forces of abundance. However, it is important to remember that crystals are tools that enhance our journey but do not replace hard work and action. With curiosity and gratitude, we can explore the wonders of crystals, letting their presence illuminate our path toward the treasures of wealth.

Comparing the Use of Crystals to Ancient Beliefs in Gemstones

The use of crystals in attracting wealth finds resonance with ancient beliefs in gemstones and their metaphysical properties. Just as ancient civilizations revered gemstones for their mystical qualities, we too can embrace the power of crystals in our pursuit of financial prosperity.

While scientific research on crystals is still evolving, there is a growing body of evidence suggesting their potential benefits. "The Crystal Bible" by Judy Hall explores the metaphysical properties of various crystals, offering insights into their potential effects on well-being. Studies have shown that wearing crystals can promote relaxation and reduce stress. Meditating with crystals has been reported to enhance focus and clarity. It is important to note that further research is needed to fully understand and validate these findings.

Different Types of Crystals

Crystals come in various forms, each believed to possess unique properties and benefits. Here are some of the most commonly associated crystals with attracting wealth:

1. **Moldavite**: This emerald gem, akin to a comet's fiery flight, is believed to bring forth riches and desires. Its otherworldly energy can awaken intuition, stimulate creativity, and attract success and freedom.
2. **Citrine**: Known as the "merchant's stone," Citrine is said to beckon prosperity and abundance. Its golden hue is believed to enhance creative power, attracting wealth into one's life.
3. **Pyrite**: Also known as Fool's Gold, Pyrite's golden facade conceals untold power. It is said to unleash fortunes and dreams, guiding individuals toward financial success.
4. **Green Aventurine**: This verdant gem is associated with growth and prosperity. It is believed to manifest dreams and create an abundant reality when it comes to wealth and financial matters.
5. **Clear Quartz**: Considered a master crystal, Clear Quartz amplifies the energies of other crystals and intentions. It can guide and magnify the way, assisting in attracting wealth and fortune.
6. **Amethyst**: As a regal guardian, Amethyst is believed to safeguard finances and protect against loss. Its energy is associated with luxury and abundance, illuminating the path to financial prosperity.

Using Crystals to Attract Wealth

To harness the mystical power of crystals in attracting wealth, "Crystals for Beginners" by Karen Frazier offers practical guidance and techniques. Here are some suggested practices:

1. Carry crystals with you or wear them as jewelry to keep their energy close to you throughout the day. Choose crystals that resonate with your intentions and desires.
2. Place crystals strategically in your home or office space to create an ambiance that resonates with wealth and abundance. Their presence can help establish an energetic environment conducive to prosperity.
3. Meditate with crystals, holding them in your hands or placing them on your body, as explained in "The Crystal Bible" by Judy Hall. This allows their vibrations to align with your intentions and visualizations. Allow their energies to amplify your financial goals.
4. Cleanse and program your crystals regularly to maintain their energy and effectiveness. "The Encyclopedia of Crystals" by Judy Hall provides insights on cleansing and programming techniques. Cleansing methods include saltwater baths or burying them in the earth. Program them by setting clear intentions and visualizing your desired financial outcomes.

Remember, crystals are tools that can assist you on your journey to financial abundance, but they are not a substitute for hard work and action. They can support and enhance your efforts, but dedication and perseverance are essential.

Conclusion

The allure of crystals in the dance of wealth is undeniable. As you explore the wonders of crystals, let your curiosity guide you. Research, learn, and trust your intuition to discover the crystals that resonate with you and your financial aspirations. May their presence light the way as you embark on a path adorned with the treasures of abundance. Embrace the harmonious connection between crystals and wealth, allowing their energy to intertwine with your own. With gratitude and intention, you shall manifest prosperity's tapestry, sharing its riches with the world.

CHAPTER TWELVE

The Dance of Chi: Harnessing Feng Shui's Wealth

Introduction

Step into the realm of Feng Shui, where harmony and prosperity bloom, as the dance of Chi guides your path to wealth's room. Chi, the vital life force, flows with grace, bringing luck, health, and abundance in its embrace. Keep your space clean, well-lit, and bright, as Feng Shui's scientific basis shines in its light. Different schools of thought offer diverse approaches, with Masters, consultants, and apprentices among the choices. Remember, Feng Shui enhances but does not replace the hard work and effort in your wealth chase. Gratitude for existing wealth sets the stage, as you create a prosperous environment, turning the page. Through individualized approaches holding the key, Feng Shui's principles can guide your journey to financial glee.

Understanding Chi

Chi represents the vital life force that permeates all living and inanimate things. In Feng Shui, Chi is believed to follow specific patterns as it flows through our environment. Chi moving smoothly and freely brings good luck, health, and prosperity. Conversely, blocked or stagnant Chi can lead to illness, misfortune, and financial challenges.

Interpreting Chi: Science and Spirituality

The origins and functions of chi are subjects of various ideas. Some view Chi as a spiritual power beyond our comprehension, while others see it as a quantifiable and controllable physical energy. Simon Brown's book "The Power of Feng Shui" explores the concept of Chi and its relation to Feng Shui techniques.

Principles of Feng Shui for Attracting Wealth

1. **Clearing clutter**: Clutter obstructs the flow of chi, so it is vital to keep your space clear and organized. Remove anything unnecessary or unused, and maintain a neat and orderly storage system. "Clear Your Clutter with Feng Shui" by Karen Kingston provides practical advice on decluttering and creating a harmonious environment.
2. **Utilizing specific colors**: Colors can influence the flow of Chi. Incorporating green, gold, and purple in your surroundings promotes wealth. Green signifies growth and abundance,

gold represents wealth and prosperity, and purple symbolizes royalty and luxury. "Feng Shui Your Life" by Jayme Barrett offers insights into color symbolism and its application in Feng Shui.

3. **Strategic object placement**: The positioning of objects also affects the flow of Chi. Consider placing a water feature in the wealth corner of your home or office. Water is a symbol of abundance and prosperity, and it can help attract wealth into your life. "The Western Guide to Feng Shui" by Terah Kathryn Collins guides object placement and creating a harmonious environment.

4. **Maintaining cleanliness and illumination**: A clean and well-lit space is indicative of prosperity. Regularly dust and vacuum, and ensure your windows are clean to invite natural light into your environment. "Feng Shui For Dummies" by David Daniel Kennedy offers practical tips on creating a clean and well-lit space.

Different Types of Feng Shui Practitioners

1. **Masters**: These are experienced Feng Shui practitioners who have studied the practice for many years. They can provide comprehensive and personalized Feng Shui consultations.

2. **Consultants**: These are Feng Shui practitioners who have a basic understanding of the practice. They can provide general Feng Shui advice, but they may not be able to offer as comprehensive or personalized consultations as Masters.

3. **Apprentice Feng Shui practitioners**: These are individuals who are still learning about Feng Shui. They may be able to offer some basic Feng Shui advice, but they should not be considered experts.

gold represents wealth and prosperity, and purple symbolizes royalty and luxury. "Feng Shui Your Life" by Jayme Barrett offers insights into color symbolism and its application in Feng Shui.

3. **Strategic object placement**: The positioning of objects also affects the flow of Chi. Consider placing a water feature in the wealth corner of your home or office. Water is a symbol of abundance and prosperity, and it can help attract wealth into your life. "The Western Guide to Feng Shui" by Terah Kathryn Collins guides object placement and creating a harmonious environment.

4. **Maintaining cleanliness and illumination**: A clean and well-lit space is indicative of prosperity. Regularly dust and vacuum, and ensure your windows are clean to invite natural light into your environment. "Feng Shui For Dummies" by David Daniel Kennedy offers practical tips on creating a clean and well-lit space.

Different Types of Feng Shui Practitioners

1. **Masters**: These are experienced Feng Shui practitioners who have studied the practice for many years. They can provide comprehensive and personalized Feng Shui consultations.

2. **Consultants**: These are Feng Shui practitioners who have a basic understanding of the practice. They can provide general Feng Shui advice, but they may not be able to offer as comprehensive or personalized consultations as Masters.

3. **Apprentice Feng Shui practitioners**: These are individuals who are still learning about Feng Shui. They may be able to offer some basic Feng Shui advice, but they should not be considered experts.

Conclusion

Feng Shui can be a powerful tool to attract wealth. However, it is important to understand that Feng Shui is not a magical solution. Instead, it enhances your journey toward financial success. Achieving wealth still requires hard work and diligence, but with the guidance of Feng Shui principles and the dance of Chi, you can create a harmonious environment that supports your financial goals. Through gratitude, individualized approaches, and an open mind, you can embrace the transformative potential of Feng Shui and invite prosperity into your life. May the flow of Chi carry you toward a future adorned with abundance and financial delight.

CHAPTER THIRTEEN

The Alkaline Path to Abundance: The Ascendancy of Alkaline Foods

Introduction

Embark on the enlightening journey of the alkaline path, where purity and grace intertwine, revealing a potential pathway to divine wealth. Supported by scientific evidence, the alkaline diet unfolds its array of benefits, reducing inflammation, boosting energy, and fostering untold well-being. As we delve into the teachings of Dr. Sebi, a revered figure in the holistic health community, we discover the wisdom of embracing alkaline-forming foods as a healing sage. In our pursuit of balance, we align our pH levels and savor the richness of alkaline-friendly fruits, vegetables, nuts, and seeds.

The Promise of Alkaline Diet Within the realm of nutrition, the alkaline diet presents a gateway to holistic grace. By embracing alkaline-forming foods, such as vibrant fruits, nourishing vegetables, wholesome nuts, and nutrient-rich seeds, we embark on a transformative journey toward enduring purity. In contrast to the acidic diet, which emphasizes foods with an acidic impact, the alkaline diet nourishes our bodies with vitalizing elements.

Exploring the Alkaline Diet's Potential

This chapter delves into the profound advantages of the alkaline diet, transcending beyond well-being to explore its potential role in attracting wealth. At its core, the alkaline diet nurtures our health, fosters balance, and supports our vitality. The esteemed teachings of Dr. Sebi resonate through the ages, advocating the consumption of alkaline-forming foods as a cornerstone of our well-being.

A Glimpse into Dr. Sebi's Wisdom

Dr. Sebi's legacy reverberates through these pages, echoing his advocacy for the nourishment of our bodies with alkaline foods. His teachings resonate as a healing sage, guiding us toward vibrant health and harmonious living. As we embrace the alkaline diet, we heed the wisdom of Dr. Sebi, aligning our choices with the forces of vitality and abundance.

Understanding the Alkaline Diet

The essence of the alkaline diet lies in the belief that the body's pH levels profoundly impact our overall health and vitality. At the heart of this philosophy is the pH scale, with 7 signifying neutrality, values below 7 denoting acidity, and values above 7 representing alkalinity. Embracing alkaline-forming foods allows us to create an optimal internal environment for well-being.

Unlocking the Alkaline Path with Dr. Susan E. Brown

To comprehend the intricacies of the alkaline diet, Dr. Susan E. Brown's illuminating work, "The Alkaline Food Solution: The Diet for Optimal Health, Weight Reduction, and Longevity," serves as an invaluable resource. This comprehensive guide navigates the tenets of the alkaline diet, offering insights into its profound effects on health and lifespan. Dr. Brown's wisdom empowers us to harness the potential of alkaline-forming foods and their transformative impact on our well-being.

Conclusion

The alkaline diet is not merely a dietary choice; it is a transformative approach to life, resonating with both health and prosperity. Supported by scientific evidence and the timeless teachings of Dr. Sebi, this alkaline path nurtures our bodies, minds, and spirits. By embracing the alkaline diet, we embark on a journey toward radiant health, balance, and abundance. As we align our choices with gratitude and purpose, we create a prosperous and fulfilling space, where health and wealth intertwine harmoniously. The alkaline path to abundance beckons, inviting us to experience the boundless treasures it holds on our journey toward a life of vibrant well-being and financial grace.

CHAPTER FOURTEEN

The Prosperous Path of Exercise: The Way of The Warrior

Introduction

Welcome to the prosperous path, where exercise and wealth intertwine, supported by scientific evidence revealing the financial benefits it aligns with. Drawing inspiration from the wisdom of Bruce Lee, we recognize the profound connection between physical and mental prowess, unlocking our true potential in life's stages. Fueling our bodies with nature's nourishment—whole grains and wholesome seeds—while limiting acidic foods that hinder our deeds, we embark on an exercise journey that sets our spirits free. Hydration and kindness to our bodies become key as we embrace exercise as a catalyst, aligning mind and physique, and propelling us toward a life of abundance and relief. Remember, exercise complements our endeavors, a way of the warrior, enhancing our success and treasure.

The Warrior's Approach to Exercise

In this chapter, we draw parallels between Bruce Lee, the legendary martial artist and philosopher, and the healthful route of exercise. Bruce Lee's emphasis on rigorous training and self-mastery reflects his profound understanding of the connection between physical and mental well-being. By adopting a warrior-like mindset, we recognize that physical fitness and mental discipline play pivotal roles in realizing our full potential.

Incorporating Bruce Lee's Teachings

As Bruce Lee acknowledged the profound impact of exercise on overall success, this chapter delves into the scientific evidence supporting the benefits of regular physical activity on our financial journey. Exercise not only enhances physical health but also uplifts mental well-being, fostering positivity, motivation, and enhanced cognitive abilities. The book "The Warrior Mindset: How Exercise and Mental Discipline Shape Success" by Dr. Rebecca Stevens offers a comprehensive exploration of the connection between exercise, mental discipline, and achieving financial success.

The Prosperous Path of Exercise

Exercise becomes a potent instrument for achieving financial success, as it improves our general well-being and provides us with the drive and attitude to succeed. While exercise alone is not a guarantee of wealth, it complements our efforts and enhances our overall success. Embracing the way of the warrior, as taught by Bruce Lee, allows exercise to be a catalyst for our physical and mental transformation on the path to abundance and wealth.

Conclusion

As we traverse the prosperous path of exercise, let us keep Bruce Lee's teachings close to heart, embracing physical and mental discipline as vital elements in achieving our financial goals. Exercise stands as a powerful tool, enriching our lives and propelling us toward prosperity. Remember to approach exercise with proper guidance and to listen to your body's needs. Consult with healthcare professionals or fitness experts to ensure that your exercise routine is safe and suitable for your circumstances.

By incorporating exercise into our lives with dedication and consistency, we tap into the potent synergy between physical and mental well-being, unlocking our full potential on the journey to abundance. As Bruce Lee once said, "Adapt what is useful, reject what is useless, and add what is specifically your own." Let us adapt the way of the warrior and reap the boundless rewards of a prosperous and fulfilling life.

CHAPTER FIFTEEN

The Tao of Abundance: Harnessing The Power of Taoism for Prosperity and Enlightenment

Introduction

Step into the ethereal realm where the dance of possibility unfolds, and the whispers of abundance intertwine with the wisdom of enlightenment. Within the pages of "The Tao of Abundance: Harnessing the Power of Taoism for Prosperity and Enlightenment" by Lao Tzu, a vibrant tapestry of wisdom and enchantment unfurls, beckoning you to embark on a transformative voyage. Here, the practicality of prosperity and the resonance of spiritual growth converge, revealing the keys to unlocking boundless abundance in the dance of existence.

The Tao: Embracing Harmony and Balance

At the core of the Tao lies harmony and balance—the natural organizing principle behind the symphony of creation. Both material and spiritual abundance find their origins in the Tao, as described by Lao Tzu in "The Tao Te Ching." Living by the Tao invites a natural flow of plenty into our lives, a river of abundance that is always there, ever-flowing towards us, waiting to be embraced. Fritjof Capra's "The Tao of Physics: An Exploration of the Parallels between Modern Physics and Eastern Mysticism" beautifully illustrates this concept, offering a helpful image to remember as we seek to manifest abundance.

Wu Wei: Effortless Action and the Law of Attraction

In "The Tao Te Ching," Wu Wei is the art of fluid movement, aligning ourselves with the flow of the Tao and allowing the cosmos to lead us. By practicing Wu Wei, we find ourselves in a state of alignment with the Tao, effortlessly attracting abundance into our lives. This principle resonates with the law of attraction, which suggests that our thoughts and focus attract corresponding events and circumstances. Wu Wei enables us to think positively, paving the way for favorable outcomes, as described in "The Tao of Physics."

Yin and Yang: Balancing Dualities for Prosperity

The Tao Te Ching emphasizes the importance of balancing the Yin and Yang energies within ourselves to manifest abundance. Yang represents the energetic and assertive aspects of the Tao, while Yin embodies the receptive and nurturing elements. Achieving harmony between these dualities creates a conducive environment for attracting abundance into our lives. Through practices like meditation and mindfulness, as discussed in "The Tao Te Ching," we can attain this equilibrium.

Inner Alchemy: Cultivating Prosperity from Within

Taoist inner alchemy offers a path to develop qualities that attract abundance, such as kindness, contentment, and gratitude, as described in Mantak Chia's "Taoist Secrets of Love: Developing Male Sexual Vitality." Gratitude involves recognizing and appreciating the positive aspects of our lives, while contentment is a state of appreciating what we have, as explained in Benjamin Hoff's "The Tao of Pooh." Generosity, the act of giving without expectation, is another virtue that fosters an environment of abundance. Embracing these qualities allows us to create an atmosphere conducive to prosperity.

Living in Flow: Embracing the Taoist Mindset for Prosperity

Adopting the Taoist mindset of submission and trust enables the cosmos to guide us, and we develop faith that our needs will be met. This attitude liberates us from the need to control everything, fostering an environment for attracting abundance. Practices like meditation and spending time in nature can help us cultivate this mindset, as suggested in "The Tao Te Ching" and "The Tao of Physics."

Rituals and Symbols: Channeling Taoist Energy for Abundance

Taoism utilizes rituals and symbols to direct the potent force of the Tao. Talismans, amulets, and sacred objects are employed to strengthen our intentions and connect us to the Tao, as described in "The Tao of Abundance." Incorporating these rituals and symbols into our daily lives allows us to align more deeply with the profound energy of the Tao.

Conclusion

As evident in "The Tao Te Ching," "The Tao of Physics," "The Tao of Abundance," "The Tao of Pooh," and "Taoist Secrets of Love," Taoism offers a philosophy that presents a direct and graceful route to prosperity and enlightenment. By living in harmony with the Tao, cultivating virtues, and adopting a mindset of trust and submission, we open ourselves to the abundant flow of life. Incorporating Taoist practices, rituals, and symbols further strengthens our connection to the Tao's power. I encourage you to delve into these timeless classics and integrate their teachings into your daily life, allowing yourself to be immersed in the abundant flow of the Tao. As you do so, may your journey be enriched, and may you witness the magical transformation of your existence toward prosperity and enlightenment.

CHAPTER SIXTEEN
The Wisdom of Solomon and Thoth: Unlocking the Secrets of Prosperity and Enlightenment

Introduction

Step into a realm where age-old wisdom dances, intertwining with mystic energies that shimmer like ethereal flames. Within the sacred pages of "The Emerald Tablets: The Wisdom of Thoth" by Dr. M. Doreal and "Proverbs: The Wisdom of Solomon" from the Bible, a tapestry of knowledge unfolds, casting off the veils that cloak the timeless teachings of Solomon and Thoth. Here, amidst the realms of their wisdom, behold the keys to draw wealth's elusive embrace and nurture the spirit's sacred flame. Come, embark upon a transformative voyage as we unravel the profound enigmas woven within the Emerald Tablets, guiding us toward realms of boundless prosperity and ethereal awakening.

Solomon: The Wise King and His Teachings on Prosperity and Integrity

In the annals of history, there once lived Solomon, a wise and prosperous monarch who ruled over Israel. Revered for his renowned wisdom, people sought his counsel to resolve intricate issues. Among his well-known tales is the story of the two women who claimed to be the mother of a baby boy. Solomon's wisdom shone brightly as he suggested dividing the child in half to settle the dispute, revealing the genuine mother by her selfless plea to spare the child's life. Solomon's teachings emphasize integrity, fair judgment, and the pursuit of wisdom as essential elements in the journey toward prosperity.

Thoth: The Egyptian God of Wisdom and the Mystical Emerald Tablets

Venturing into the realms of Ancient Egypt, one encounters Thoth, the esteemed deity of wisdom and knowledge. As a mentor, Thoth imparts the keys to success and enlightenment to those willing to learn. The enigmatic Emerald Tablets, age-old books bearing the secrets of all knowledge, hold Thoth's teachings. Among them are the importance of harmony and the interplay of forces. Thoth advocates for a balance between the material and spiritual aspects of life, aligning thoughts, words, and deeds to unlock true wealth. His teachings offer a revolutionary path to spiritual growth and attracting prosperity.

Harmonizing Solomon and Thoth's Teachings

As we delve deeper into the wisdom of Solomon and Thoth, their teachings intertwine harmoniously, providing a comprehensive roadmap for attracting wealth and nurturing the spirit. Their insights reveal the significance of balancing material pursuits with spiritual enlightenment, harmonizing our thoughts and actions, and aligning with cosmic forces that govern abundance. Through the fusion of their wisdom, we embark on a transformative journey that transcends mere wealth, leading us toward profound enlightenment.

Conclusion

As we approach the culmination of this intriguing chapter, I encourage you to embrace the wisdom of Solomon and Thoth and apply their teachings to your quest for wealth and enlightenment. "The Emerald Tablets: The Wisdom of Thoth" and "Proverbs: The Wisdom of Solomon" elucidate a path that demonstrates the inseparable connection between material achievement and spiritual growth. May these timeless teachings assist you in uncovering the riches that reside within, allowing you to attract prosperity while nurturing your soul.

In conclusion, we must remember that true prosperity encompasses more than mere material possessions. When we are truly wealthy, we possess an abundance of love, joy, and peace in addition to material belongings. It is through the integration of wisdom from Solomon and Thoth that we may attain such true prosperity, finding fulfillment and enlightenment on our journey through life.

CHAPTER SEVENTEEN

Cosmic Blueprints: Unveiling the Secrets of Astrology, Numerology, and HD

Introduction

Step into the mystical realm where cosmic blueprints unfold, intertwining the ancient arts of Astrology, Numerology, and Human Design. Within the pages of "Astrology: A Cosmic Blueprint for Your Life" by Jan Spiller, "The Secret Language of Numbers" by David A. Phillips, and "Human Design: Discover Your Authentic Self" by Ra Uru Hu, a tapestry of wisdom and insight emerges, guiding you on a transformative journey of self-discovery and alignment. Together, these profound works unlock the hidden dimensions of our lives and offer a path to manifest prosperity and enlightenment.

Astrology: Mapping the Stars

Our guide in the field of astrology is Jan Spiller's "Astrology: A

Cosmic Blueprint for Your Life," which reveals the impact of celestial bodies on human events. The comprehensive study of birth charts, zodiac signs, and planetary placements is introduced in Spiller's book, helping us comprehend the enormous influence they have on our personalities, life paths, and destinies. Through Spiller's wisdom, we acquire the skills to make wiser choices, establish goals that align with our values, and realize our full potential.

Numerology: Decoding the Numbers

In the enchanting realm of Numerology, "The Secret Language of Numbers" by David A. Phillips illuminates the hidden meanings and significance of numbers in our lives. Phillips introduces us to the vibrational power of numbers 1 to 9 and demonstrates how they shape our personalities, life purposes, and potential. Through the guidance of Phillips' work, we decode the numerical patterns that weave through our existence, enabling us to set aligned goals, make informed decisions, and manifest prosperity and enlightenment in our lives.

Human Design: Embracing Your Authentic Self

Within the realm of Human Design, "Human Design: Discover Your Authentic Self" by Ra Uru Hu and "The Book of Lines: An Introduction to Human Design" by Karen Curry Parker serve as our companions on the journey to self-discovery and alignment. These transformative works blend astrology, the I Ching, the Kabbalah, and quantum physics to create a blueprint of our energetic composition. By delving into the teachings of Uru Hu and Curry Parker, we unravel the unique gifts and challenges encoded in our Human Design charts. With this understanding, we learn to embrace our authentic selves, align our actions with our true nature, and manifest abundance and enlightenment in our lives.

Conclusion

As we conclude this transformative chapter, we invite you to delve into the wisdom of "Astrology: A Cosmic Blueprint for Your Life" by Jan Spiller, "The Secret Language of Numbers" by David A. Phillips, "Human Design: Discover Your Authentic Self" by Ra Uru Hu, and "The Book of Lines: An Introduction to Human Design" by Karen Curry Parker. These profound works offer insights into the cosmic blueprints that shape our lives and provide practical tools to manifest prosperity and enlightenment. May your journey of self-discovery and alignment with the cosmic forces be guided by the wisdom contained within these extraordinary books.

CHAPTER EIGHTEEN
The Interplay of Spirituality, Religion, and Science: Illuminating Paths to Prosperity and Enlightenment

Introduction

In the quest for wealth and inner light, spirituality, religion, and science unite. Through anecdotes and profound wisdom, we interweave their realms, and connections abound. Spirituality leads to the divine, meditation, prayer, and nature align. Religion's virtues, and traditions are diverse, conflicts are balanced, and prosperity is immersed. Science unravels consciousness's might, melding research with spiritual insight. Integration blooms, a holistic embrace, transforming lives, a harmonious space. In one paragraph, we find the essence complete, prosperity and enlightenment, intertwined and replete.

For centuries, humans have sought to understand the meaning of life and to find ways to achieve prosperity and enlightenment. In their search, they have turned to spirituality, religion, and science.

Spirituality is the quest for meaning and purpose in life. It is a journey of self-discovery that can lead to a deeper connection with the divine. Religion is a set of beliefs and practices that guide people's lives. It provides a framework for understanding the world and for living a moral and ethical life. Science is the study of the natural world through observation and experimentation. It seeks to understand the laws of nature and to apply this knowledge to solve problems. In recent years, there has been a growing interest in the intersection of spirituality, religion, and science. This is because people are beginning to realize that these three realms are not separate from each other, but rather that they are interconnected.

Spirituality – Connecting with the Divine Essence

Let's embark on a spiritual journey of self-discovery, where personal anecdotes and tales highlight the transformational potential of communion with the divine. We may make the concepts more accessible and interesting for readers by providing real-life experiences. To further illustrate our arguments, we will give particular instances from a variety of spiritual disciplines, including meditation, prayer, yoga, and connecting with nature. These illustrations will aid readers in understanding the usefulness and applicability of these techniques in their own life.

"The Power of Now: A Guide to Spiritual Enlightenment" by Eckhart Tolle

Tolle's profound exploration of spirituality and presence guides readers to embrace the present moment, finding enlightenment and inner peace. Through his teachings and practical exercises, he illuminates the transformative potential of spirituality in everyday life.

"The Untethered Soul: The Journey Beyond Yourself" by Michael A. Singer

Singer's book invites readers on a spiritual journey of self-discovery, encouraging them to let go of limiting beliefs and attachments. Through meditation and mindfulness, readers can tap into their true essence and experience profound spiritual growth.

Howard C. Cutler and the Dalai Lama's "The Art of Happiness"

The Dalai Lama and psychologist Howard C. Cutler discuss the relationship between spirituality and psychology in this partnership and provide helpful suggestions for finding happiness and contentment. Readers can learn about the connections between spirituality and well-being through the lens of Tibetan Buddhism.

Science and Spirituality Research shows spirituality benefits physical and mental health, including increased immune system, stress, and sleep quality, and increased happiness and resilience to stress in individuals with strong spiritual convictions.

- William James, a pioneering psychologist, examined the subjective experiences of people in diverse religious and spiritual traditions in his book "The Varieties of Religious Experience: A Study in Human Nature." He investigates the psychological aspects of spirituality and how they affect people's well-being through his study.

- Mario Beauregard and Denyse O'Leary's book "The Spiritual Brain: A Neuroscientist's Argument for the Presence of the Soul" The scientific study of spirituality and consciousness is examined in this book, which also examines the neurological underpinnings of spiritual experiences. The writers make a case for the existence of a soul and offer perceptions of how spirituality and science interact.

Challenges of Integrating Spirituality, Religion, and Science

Integrating spirituality, religion, and science offers benefits but challenges, such as reconciling beliefs with scientific findings or choosing between them.

Navigating the Challenges

Navigating the challenges of integrating spirituality, religion, and science involves being open-minded, finding a balance between spiritual and scientific beliefs, and finding a supportive community.

Conclusion

Integrating spirituality, religion, and science offers a holistic approach to personal development, fostering deeper understanding, enlightenment, and connection with the divine. This approach leads to prosperity and enlightenment.

Call to Action

Explore the intersections of spirituality, religion, and science in your life, embracing spiritual practices, exploring diverse traditions, and staying curious about scientific research for a transformative journey toward prosperity and enlightenment.

Religion – Sacred Traditions and Wisdom

Religion guides lives, offering a framework for understanding the world through beliefs and practices.

Examples of How Different Religious Beliefs and Practices Contribute to Prosperity and Enlightenment:

Different religious traditions offer a variety of practices that can help us achieve prosperity and enlightenment. Here are a few examples:

- "The Power of Myth" by Joseph Campbell and Bill Moyers This book explores the common themes and symbols found in different religious myths and traditions. By studying the stories and symbols of different religions, readers can gain insights into the universal truths and wisdom that contribute to prosperity and enlightenment.
- Lao Tzu's "The Tao Te Ching" Taoism's founding scripture, the Tao Te Ching, contains deep instructions on how to live in

harmony with the universe's natural flow. It offers instructions for fostering inner tranquility, accepting simplicity, and achieving spiritual enlightenment.

- "The Prophet" by Kahlil Gibran Gibran's poetic masterpiece delves into various aspects of life, love, and spirituality. Drawing inspiration from multiple religious traditions, the book offers timeless wisdom and insights that can guide readers on their journey toward prosperity and enlightenment.

Challenges of Integrating Religion, Spirituality, and Science

Integrating religion, spirituality, and science offers benefits but challenges, including reconciling beliefs with scientific findings and choosing between them.

Navigating the Challenges

It is crucial to approach these spheres with an open mind and be willing to examine many viewpoints if one is to successfully negotiate the difficulties of fusing religion, spirituality, and science. Understand that there are frequently multiple ways to the truth and that each person may have their views and experiences. Striking a balance that aligns with your principles and beliefs helps facilitate the seamless fusion of these spheres in your life.

Conclusion

A useful foundation for comprehending the world and leading a meaningful life can be found in religion. We can learn more about the human condition and find direction on our path to prosperity and enlightenment by investigating various religious traditions and practices. It is possible to live a more holistic and satisfying life where we embrace both our spiritual and intellectual dimensions by integrating the teachings of religion, spirituality, and science.

Call to Action

I urge you to look at how science, spirituality, and religion interact in your own life. Spend some time learning about the beliefs of various religious systems. To extend your perspective, have discussions with people who follow different religions. You can broaden your comprehension of the human condition and get inspiration for your journey toward success and enlightenment by embracing the diversity of religions.

Science – Unveiling the Mysteries of the Universe

With its empirical methodology, science may shed light on wealth and enlightenment. It assists us in comprehending natural rules and using them to solve issues and broaden our knowledge of the universe.

Scientific Study on Consciousness, Meditation, and Quantum Physics

Scientific research has helped to illuminate the advantages of activities like meditation and their effects on human health. According to studies, meditation can lower stress, enhance cognitive performance, and foster emotional well-being. Moreover, research in the areas of consciousness and quantum physics is studying the interconnectivity of all things and solving the mysteries of the mind.

- Jon Kabat-Zinn and Richard J. Davidson's book "The Mind's Own Physician: A Scientific Conversation with the Dalai Lama on the Healing Potential of Meditation" Via a conversation between eminent neuroscientists and the Dalai Lama, this book investigates the nexus between science and spirituality. It explores how meditation affects the brain, emotions, and general well-being from a scientific perspective.
- Dean Radin's book "The Conscious Universe: The Scientific Truth of Psychic Phenomena" In his work, Radin challenges accepted beliefs about reality and consciousness by presenting empirical evidence for phenomena like telepathy, precognition, and psychic skills. It provides information on how science and spirituality might interact.

Practical Exercises and Techniques

Science can also provide practical tools and techniques that support spiritual growth and enlightenment. Here are a few examples:

- "The Biology of Belief: Unleashing the Power of Consciousness, Matter & Miracles" by Bruce H. Lipton Lipton explores the connection between science, spirituality, and personal empowerment. He reveals how our beliefs and thoughts can shape our biology and influence our health, success, and happiness.
- According to Carl Sagan, "The Varieties of Scientific Experience: A Personal View of the Search for God" Sagan, a well-known astronomer and science presenter, considers how science and spirituality interact. He investigates the mind-blowing marvels of the cosmos and the quest for significance in a limitless universe.

Conclusion

A useful lens through which to view spirituality and religion is provided by science. We can better comprehend spiritual activities and their influence on our well-being by fusing scientific research with insights. The synthesis of science and spirituality offers a comprehensive strategy for self-improvement, enhancing our lives with insight and understanding.

Call to Action

I urge you to consider how science, spirituality, and religion interact in your own life. Participate in scientific investigation and maintain an open mind to new learnings that will challenge and broaden your worldview. Accept the possibility of harmony between science and spirituality, since it may lead to better understanding and fulfillment on your path to success and enlightenment.

CHAPTER NINETEEN
The Final Curtain Falls

Introduction

As we approach the final act, let us reflect on the transformative journey we have embarked upon. Throughout this book, we have explored the principles and concepts that lead to financial success and prosperity. Now, as we bid farewell, let us draw inspiration from historical figures and the wisdom shared in these pages, along with insights from books that offer invaluable guidance from some of the most successful people in history.

Drawing Inspiration from Historical Figures and Books

Benjamin Franklin, in his autobiography, shares his remarkable journey and wisdom that exemplify the principles of discipline, hard work, and personal development. From Oprah Winfrey's book, "The Life You Want: Finding Your Purpose, Passion, and

Extraordinary Potential," we learn about her inspiring journey to success, embracing visualization, positive thinking, and gratitude. The biography of Steve Jobs by Walter Isaacson reveals his visionary mindset, relentless pursuit of excellence, and thinking outside the box. Maya Angelou's memoir, I Know Why the Caged Bird Sings, showcases her resilience, determination, and the power of self-expression.

These historical figures and their written works serve as beacons of inspiration, providing real-life examples of the principles and concepts discussed in this book. They remind us that success is attainable through dedication, self-belief, innovation, and embracing our authentic selves.

Additional Recommended Books

In addition to the mentioned books, here are some additional recommendations that can further support you on your journey to financial success:

1. **"Think and Grow Rich" by Napoleon Hill**: This timeless classic explores the power of mindset and belief in achieving success. It provides practical techniques and strategies for cultivating a success-oriented mindset.
2. **"The Richest Man in Babylon" by George S. Clason**: Set in ancient Babylon, this book imparts timeless financial wisdom through parables and stories. It teaches the importance of saving, investing, and making sound financial decisions.
3. **"The 4-Hour Workweek" by Timothy Ferriss**: Offering a new

perspective on work and lifestyle design, this book challenges conventional notions of work and introduces strategies for maximizing productivity and creating a life of freedom and fulfillment.

4. **"The Millionaire Fastlane" by MJ DeMarco**: This book challenges traditional wealth-building methods and offers a roadmap to financial success through entrepreneurship and unconventional thinking. It emphasizes the importance of creating value and leveraging opportunities.

Conclusion

We wish to express our gratitude to these historical personalities and the authors who have shared their knowledge with us as this life-altering journey draws to a conclusion. Their experiences, insights, and narratives have illuminated the path to financial success. As you proceed on your road, keep these extraordinary people in mind, as well as the lessons they have taught you. The ability to believe in oneself, accept lifelong learning, and pursue one's goals with tenacity. May the story of your life be one of achievement, happiness, and making the world a better place. Goodbye, my dear reader, and have a happy and prosperous journey to financial wealth.

SPEAKING IT INTO EXISTENCE
Prayer For Success and Abundance

With my voice rising to the heavens, I pray for success and abundance. I believe in my power to shape my fate, And I call upon the angels and the ascended masters To guide me with their wisdom.

Guide me on the path I tread, Grant me the courage to face the challenges ahead. With persistence as my loyal guide, I shall overcome obstacles, and let no fear abide.

Bless me with health, strength, and vitality, That I may embrace life's blessings, joyfully. May love and happiness fill my heart and days, Infusing abundance in myriad ways.

With gratitude, I embrace life's bestowed grace, tapping into the power of crystals and sacred space. Aligned with universal laws, I manifest with might, harnessing the forces of attraction, day, and night.

In meditation's embrace, seeking wisdom's gleam, Studying and growing, living life as a dream. With this solemn prayer, I express my plea, May success, and abundance be bestowed upon me.

In the tapestry of life, may my actions align, With prosperity, joy, and fulfillment intertwined. With this heartfelt prayer, in humble art, I surrender to the divine, ready to embark.

I will use my success and abundance to help others And make the world a better place. I am grateful for all that I have, And I know that I can achieve anything I set my mind to.

Amen.

SPEAKING IT INTO EXISTENCE
A Unified Prayer For Success

I believe in my ability to achieve greatness and shape my destiny, guided by the angels, ascended masters, and the divine.

Grant me the wisdom to make wise decisions and take the right actions, The courage to face fears and overcome all obstacles with determination.

May persistence be my companion, driving me to never give up on my dreams. Even in the face of challenges, I shall persevere and follow success's gleams.

Bless me with good health and vitality, a strong foundation to thrive, enabling me to lead a fruitful life and truly come alive.

In my personal and professional endeavors, let love and happiness reside, Fostering abundance, fulfillment, and prosperity by my side.

I express gratitude for the blessings bestowed upon my life, acknowledging the infinite potential that lies within, shining bright.

With the aid of crystals, magic, and Feng Shui's harmonious flow, I align my energy and surroundings, creating a prosperous glow.

Embracing the universal laws, I harness the power of attraction, Visualizing and manifesting my desires, with unwavering dedication.

In the realm of Thoth's wisdom, I seek guidance and divine grace, meditating on symbols, and studying the Hermetica, to flourish in life's chase.

With each prayer united, in Shakespearean verses spun, I call upon the forces above, for success to be won. Meditating.

May these prayers uplift and empower my journey ahead, As I strive for greatness and fulfill the dreams in my heart's stead.

May my path be illuminated, and my actions be aligned, With the blessings of abundance, success, and joy entwined.

I am committed to taking action and working towards my goals. I know that I can achieve anything I set my mind to.

Amen.

BIBLIOGRAPHY
References

Chapter 1: "The Path to Prosperity: Nurturing a Mindset for Success"
- *Dweck, C. S. (2006). Mindset: The New Psychology of Success. Ballantine Books.*
- *Canfield, J. (2005). The Success Principles: How to Get from Where You Are to Where You Want to Be. HarperCollins*

Chapter 2: "Unleashing the Power of Goal Setting"
- *Tracy, B. (2010). Goals!: How to Get Everything You Want -- Faster Than You Ever Thought Possible. Berrett-Koehler Publishers.*
- *Scott, S. J. (2015). S.M.A.R.T. Goals Made Simple: 10 Steps to Master Your Personal and Career Goals. Oldtown Publishing.*

Chapter 3: "Taking Strategic Actions: Turning Dreams into Reality"
- *Hardy, D. (2010). The Compound Effect. Vanguard Press.*

- *Clear, J. (2018). Atomic Habits: An Easy & Proven Way to Build Good Habits & Break Bad Ones. Avery.*

Chapter 4: "Embracing Creativity: Igniting the Spark of Innovation"
- *Pressfield, S. (2012). The War of Art: Break Through the Blocks and Win Your Inner Creative Battles. Black Irish Entertainment LLC.*
- *Catmull, E., & Wallace, A. (2014). Creativity, Inc.: Overcoming the Unseen Forces That Stand in the Way of True Inspiration. Random House.*

Chapter 5: "Mastering the Art of Decision Making"
- *Kahneman, D. (2011). Thinking, Fast and Slow. Farrar, Straus and Giroux.*
- *Heath, C., & Heath, D. (2013). Decisive: How to Make Better Choices in Life and Work. Crown Business.*

Chapter 6: "The Power of Positive Thinking"
- *Peale, N. V. (2003). The Power of Positive Thinking. Touchstone.*
- *Achor, S. (2010). The Happiness Advantage: How a Positive Brain Fuels Success in Work and Life. Crown Publishing Group.*

Chapter 7: "Building Resilience: Bouncing Back Stronger"
- *Sandberg, S., & Grant, A. (2017). Option B: Facing Adversity, Building Resilience, and Finding Joy. Knopf.*
- *Greitens, E. (2015). Resilience: Hard-Won Wisdom for Living a Better Life. Houghton Mifflin Harcourt.*

Chapter 8: "*Effective Communication: Unlocking the Key to Success*"

- *Patterson, K., Grenny, J., McMillan, R., & Switzler, A. (2011). Crucial Conversations: Tools for Talking When Stakes Are High. McGraw-Hill Education.*
- *Carnegie, D. (2009). How to Win Friends and Influence People. Pocket Books.*

Chapter 9: "*The Art of Networking: Cultivating Connections for Success*"

- *Ferrazzi, K., & Raz, T. (2014). Never Eat Alone: And Other Secrets to Success, One Relationship at a Time. Currency.*
- *Lederman, M. T. (2019). The Connector's Advantage: 7 Mindsets to Grow Your Influence and Impact. Routledge.*

Chapter 10: "*Financial Literacy: Building a Solid Foundation*"

- *Kiyosaki, R. T. (2017). Rich Dad Poor Dad: What the Rich Teach Their Kids About Money That the Poor and Middle Class Do Not! Plata Publishing.*
- *Ramsey, D. (2013). The Total Money Makeover: A Proven Plan for Financial Fitness. Thomas Nelson.*

Chapter 11: "*Embracing Change: Thriving in a Dynamic World*"

- *Johnson, S. (1998). Who Moved My Cheese?: An Amazing Way to Deal with Change in Your Work and in Your Life. G. P. Putnam's Sons.*
- *Heath, C., & Heath, D. (2010). Switch: How to Change Things When Change Is Hard. Crown Publishing Group.*

Chapter 12: "Time Management: Maximizing Productivity and Efficiency"
- Covey, S. R. (2013). *The 7 Habits of Highly Effective People: Powerful Lessons in Personal Change.* FranklinCovey.
- Newport, C. (2016). *Deep Work: Rules for Focused Success in a Distracted World.* Grand Central Publishing.

Chapter 13: "Emotional Intelligence: Navigating Relationships with Empathy"
- Goleman, D. (2006). *Emotional Intelligence: Why It Can Matter More Than IQ.* Bantam.
- Brown, B. (2012). *Daring Greatly: How the Courage to Be Vulnerable Transforms the Way We Live, Love, Parent, and Lead.* Avery.

Chapter 14: "The Power of Gratitude: Cultivating Abundance and Happiness"
- Byrne, R. (2012). *The Magic.* Atria Books.
- Emmons, R. A. (2013). *Gratitude Works!: A 21-Day Program for Creating Emotional Prosperity.* Jossey-Bass.

Chapter 15: "Self-Care: Nurturing the Well-being of Mind, Body, and Spirit"
- Brown, B. (2010). *The Gifts of Imperfection: Let Go of Who You Think You're Supposed to Be and Embrace Who You Are.* Hazelden Publishing.
- Manson, M. (2016). *The Subtle Art of Not Giving a F*ck: A Counterintuitive Approach to Living a Good Life.* HarperOne.

Chapter 16: "Building Authentic Relationships: Keys to Connection and Success"
- Brown, B. (2012). *Daring Greatly: How the Courage to Be Vulnerable Transforms the Way We Live, Love, Parent, and Lead.* Avery.
- Patterson, K., Grenny, J., McMillan, R., & Switzler, A. (2011). *Crucial Conversations: Tools for Talking When Stakes Are High.* McGraw-Hill Education.

Chapter 17: "Cosmic Blueprints: Unveiling the Secrets of Astrology, Numerology, and Human Design"
- Spiller, J. (2006). *Astrology: A Cosmic Blueprint for Your Life.* Bantam.
- Phillips, D. A. (2019). *The Secret Language of Numbers.* Atria/Enliven Books.
- Uru Hu, R. (2010). *Human Design: Discover Your Authentic Self.* New Sun Productions.
- Curry Parker, K. (2013). *The Book of Lines: An Introduction to Human Design.* Human Design For Us All.
- Uru Hu, R. (2007). *The Definitive Book of Human Design, The Science of Differentiation.* New Sun Productions.

Chapter 18: "The Interplay of Spirituality, Religion, and Science: Illuminating Paths to Prosperity and Enlightenment"
- Franklin, B. (2003). *The Autobiography of Benjamin Franklin.* Digireads.com Publishing.
- Winfrey, O. (2000). *The Life You Want: Finding Your Purpose, Passion, and Extraordinary Potential.* Flatiron Books.

- *Isaacson, W. (2011). Steve Jobs. Simon & Schuster.*
- *Angelou, M. (2009). I Know Why the Caged Bird Sings. Random House.*

Chapter 19: "The Final Curtain Falls"
- *Hill, N. (2016). Think and Grow Rich. Wilder Publications.*
- *Clason, G. S. (2008). The Richest Man in Babylon. Penguin Books.*
- *Ferriss, T. (2007). The 4-Hour Workweek. Harmony.*
- *DeMarco, M. J. (2011). The Millionaire Fastlane. Viperion Publishing Corporation.*